Mangled by a HURRICANE!

Disaster SURVIVORS

by **Miriam Aronin**

Consultant: James L. Franklin
Branch Chief, Hurricane Specialist Unit
NOAA/NWS/National Hurricane Center
Miami, Florida

BEARPORT
PUBLISHING

New York, New York

Credits

Cover, © a.isenegger/imagebroker/Alamy and © Mike Hill/Alamy; Title Page, © Mike Hill/Alamy; TOC, © Ramon Berk/Shutterstock; 4, © Eric Lease Morgan/Infomotions, Inc.; 5, © Stephen Morton/Getty Images; 6, © Kelly Owen/Zuma Press; 7T, © AP Images/Cheryl Gerber; 7B, © AP Images/Cheryl Gerber; 9T, © AP Images/Dave Martin; 9B, © AP Images/Bill Haber; 10, © Jerry Grayson/Helifilms Australia PTY Ltd/Getty Images; 11T, © Alex Brandon/The Times-Picayune/Landov; 11B, © Alex Brandon/The Times-Picayune/Landov; 12, © Mario Tama/Getty Images; 13, © Marko Georgiev/The New York Times/Redux; 14T, © AP Images/David J. Phillip; 14B, © AP Images/Paul Sancya; 15, © Mario Tama/Getty Images; 16, © Mitch Epstein/Stone/Getty Images; 17, © Dennis Hallinan/Alamy; 18, © Chris Zuppa/St. Petersburg Times/ZUMA Press; 19, © AP Images/Bill Haber; 20T, © Chad Purser/iStockphoto; 20B, © Stan Honda/AFP/Getty Images; 21, © pinecone/Shutterstock; 22, ©AP Images/Chitose Suzuki; 23L, © Skip Bolen/epa/Corbis; 23R, © AP Images/Cheryl Gerber; 24, © AP Images/Eric Gay; 25T, © AP Images/Ann Heisenfelt; 25B, © Sean Gardner/Reuters/Landov; 26T, © Trevor Booth Photography/Alamy; 26B, © David Rae Lewis/epa/Corbis; 27, © Chris Hondros/Getty Images; 28, © Maurice Rivenbark/St. Petersburg Times/ZUMA Press.

Publisher: Kenn Goin
Senior Editor: Lisa Wiseman
Creative Director: Spencer Brinker
Design: Dawn Beard Creative
Photo Researcher: Picture Perfect Professionals, LLC

Library of Congress Cataloging-in-Publication Data

Aronin, Miriam.
  Mangled by a hurricane! / by Miriam Aronin ; consultant, James L. Franklin.
    p. cm. — (Disaster survivors)
  Includes bibliographical references and index.
  ISBN-13: 978-1-936087-49-5 (lib. bdg.)
  ISBN-10: 1-936087-49-9 (lib. bdg.)
  1. Hurricanes—Juvenile literature. 2. Hurricane Katrina, 2005—Juvenile literature. I. Title.
  QC944.2.A765 2010
  551.55'2—dc22
                          2009040895

For more information, write to Bearport Publishing Company, Inc., 101 Fifth Avenue, Suite 6R, New York, New York 10003. Printed in the United States of America in North Mankato, Minnesota.

122009
090309CGE

10 9 8 7 6 5 4 3 2 1

Contents

A City in Danger

On Sunday morning, August 28, 2005, Trina Peters heard some alarming news. A powerful **hurricane** was headed straight for her home! Trina and her family lived in the Lower Ninth Ward neighborhood in New Orleans, Louisiana.

Trina's family knew how badly this kind of storm could damage the city. New Orleans is surrounded by water, mostly from the Mississippi River, Lake Pontchartrain (PON-chuhr-trayn), and the Gulf of Mexico. Many parts of the city lie on low ground close to the water. New Orleans' only protection against flooding is a system of **levees**, wall-like structures built to prevent water from coming onto the land.

A home in the Lower Ninth Ward

The levees are supposed to protect the city from storms as bad as a **Category** 3 hurricane. On Sunday, the approaching storm was a Category 5. Family members urged Trina to leave the city.

Levees such as this one were built in New Orleans after Hurricane Betsy flooded the city in 1965.

Scientists put hurricanes into five categories based on the speed of their winds. Category 1 is the weakest, with winds of up to 95 miles per hour (153 kph). Category 5 is the strongest, with winds of more than 155 miles per hour (249 kph). Storms that are rated Category 3 or higher are considered major hurricanes. However, even the weakest hurricanes can be very dangerous.

A Mighty Storm

When Trina learned about the mighty storm on Sunday, scientists had already been following it for several days. It had started on Tuesday, August 23, as a little storm in the Bahamas, a small island nation east of Florida. The next day, it had become stronger, and scientists named it **Tropical Storm** Katrina.

Katrina's winds soon built up to hurricane-strength speeds of more than 74 miles per hour (119 kph). The winds continued to increase in speed as the hurricane moved north and west toward New Orleans.

Scientists carefully watched the storm.

When a tropical storm is identified, it is given a name by the National Weather Service. The group alternates between men's and women's names. The first storm of each hurricane season gets a name starting with the letter A, the next starting with the letter B, and so on. Katrina was the 11th storm of the 2005 season.

The people of New Orleans had always feared that a tremendous hurricane would hit the city. Could this be the "Big One"? By Sunday, weather **forecasters** were warning that there could be "devastating damage" to the city once the storm hit land.

The giant storm put the home where Trina (left) lived in the Lower Ninth Ward in danger.

To prepare for the coming storm, Governor Kathleen Blanco (center) declared an emergency in Louisiana on Friday, August 26.

LandFall

    Most of Trina's family members **evacuated** their homes on Sunday. However, Trina and her 24-year-old daughter, Keia, did not want to leave their house. Some of Trina's cousins decided to stay in their homes as well. They lived just a few blocks away.

    At 6:10 A.M. on Monday, Katrina made **landfall** east of New Orleans. The winds had started to slow, but the huge storm moving toward the city was still dangerous.

Hurricane Katrina struck Florida about three days before it hit the coasts of Louisiana and Mississippi.

Hurricane Katrina's Path

As the hurricane reached New Orleans, Trina's cousins called her in terror. From their house, they could see the levees. "The water is rising," they reported. "It looks like it's about to come over the levee."

Hurricane Katrina hitting New Orleans

On Monday morning, winds of 125 miles per hour (201 kph) began uprooting trees and battering houses along the **Gulf Coast**. At the same time, a **storm surge**—made up of rising water from the sea—swept **inland**.

Rising Water

By 7:00 A.M., it was reported that water was coming over the levees in the Lower Ninth Ward. About one hour later, the area was flooded. The water had reached a height of more than six feet (1.8 m). That is taller than most adult humans.

From inside her home, Trina heard a loud noise. The pressure from the water had ripped away one wall of her house! Trina knew that she and Keia could drown as the water rose inside. However, they couldn't leave because the water outside was too deep for them to walk through. So, they scrambled onto the roof for safety.

levee

Waves from the storm surge crashed over the New Orleans levees and, in some cases, destroyed them.

Once outside, Trina and Keia saw that the wind had broken large trees and telephone poles into pieces. They saw that it had torn the roofs off other houses nearby. Trina and Keia held on to each other tightly and prayed for their lives.

A dog standing in the middle of a flooded street in the Lower Ninth Ward

Many people living in the Lower Ninth Ward found safety on the roofs of their homes.

The strongest part of Hurricane Katrina passed through New Orleans on Monday at 9:00 A.M. Even after it passed, the water continued pouring through the **breached** levees for two more days. In some parts of the city, the water was 20 feet (6 m) deep.

11

A Really Bad Dream

Not everyone who stayed in New Orleans remained in their homes. Thousands of people took shelter in the Superdome—the New Orleans football stadium.

Even inside the stadium, however, people were not out of danger. As the hurricane hit, its powerful winds ripped holes in the Superdome's roof, allowing water to leak inside. Soon, part of the roof ripped off.

More than 20,000 people had to take shelter in the Superdome. Many of them had no way to leave the city in time to escape the storm.

Conditions in the crowded stadium were horrible. There was no electricity or fresh air, and there were too few bathrooms and not enough food. Police officer David Duplantier was on duty in the Superdome. "The whole thing felt like a really bad dream," he said.

Floodwaters trapped people inside the Superdome without enough supplies.

Waiting For Help

As Trina and Keia tried to stay safe on their roof, a local fisherman used his boat to help their stranded neighbors. When he finally found Trina and Keia, he took them to an empty house nearby, where the top floor was dry.

The women waited there all night. On Tuesday, a government rescue boat finally arrived and took them to dry land.

Many people volunteered their time and their boats to help rescue people. The U.S. Coast Guard also used boats and helicopters to bring people to safety.

Many people who escaped their flooded homes were sent to the Superdome to join the others who had fled there. Conditions in the stadium got worse as the days went on. "People were starving and going without water," said television news reporter Brian Williams. By the end of the week, the U.S. government sent 30,000 soldiers to help the remaining people of New Orleans move to safer areas.

It took until Saturday, September 3, to move all the people from the Superdome to safer shelters.

It has been estimated that a little more than 1,200 people were killed by Katrina. About 1,000 of the **victims** were in Louisiana. Another 200 were in Mississippi, 6 in Florida, and 1 in Georgia.

A Hurricane Is Born

How did Katrina get its start? Like all hurricanes, it began as a group of thunderstorms over the ocean. When the ocean's **surface** is at least 80°F (27°C), large amounts of heat and **water vapor** begin moving from the ocean into the air. As heat and **moisture** rise into the **atmosphere**, clouds and thunderstorms begin to form.

As the warm air around these clouds and thunderstorms rises higher and higher, it begins to move in a spiral pattern. The speed of the spinning air increases, forming high winds. When the winds reach 39 miles per hour (63 kph), the disturbance is called a tropical storm. When they reach 74 miles per hour (119 kph), the storm is called a hurricane.

Many storms that become hurricanes in the Atlantic Ocean begin in the warm waters near the west coast of Africa.

The thunderstorms usually form a complete circle around the center of the hurricane. The center has no clouds and is called the **eye** of the storm. Usually measuring 10 to 30 miles (16 to 48 km) across, it is the calmest part. Winds are strongest at the **eyewall**, the circle of storms just outside the eye.

Katrina's eye

The Structure of a Hurricane

swirling clouds

eyewall

warm air spirals upward

eye

warm water

strong winds

The process of moving from thunderstorms to a hurricane can occur in just a couple of days.

A Stronger Storm

Katrina began like all hurricanes, but it grew to be bigger than most. Most hurricanes have a **diameter** of between 100 and 300 miles (161 and 483 km). Katrina was 440 miles (708 km) across!

Hurricane Katrina hitting Pensacola, Florida

On August 25, Katrina hit land in Florida as a Category 1 hurricane. Just three days later in the Gulf of Mexico, however, it had become a Category 5. When it finally reached Louisiana, it had weakened to a Category 3.

Hurricanes draw their strength from warm ocean waters. Storms weaken when they travel over land. Katrina became very large and powerful partly because it spent only a short amount of time over land before it hit the warm waters of the Gulf of Mexico, where winds helped the storm strengthen.

The size of the storm meant it could hit many places at once. Since it was so big, it took longer for the rain and winds to move through each area in its path. Also, large storms have a much stronger storm surge than smaller storms. Katrina's storm surge in Mississippi was 28 feet (8.5 m) high.

As the massive hurricane moved through New Orleans, its high winds blew out the windows in tall hotels, such as this one, and in office buildings.

Nothing Left

Due to its size and strength, Hurricane Katrina caused terrible damage. Alice Jackson, who lived on the Mississippi coast, had stayed with a friend during the storm. On her way home after the hurricane ended, she saw fallen power lines, toppled trees, and destroyed houses everywhere. Everything looked mangled.

More than 250,000 people had to leave their homes as a result of Hurricane Katrina.

Many homes in Mississippi were destroyed by Hurricane Katrina.

Alice was shocked when she got home. "My house was completely gone," she said. Alice was certain that she would have been killed if she had stayed inside.

Trina and Keia's house was in ruins, too. Months after the disaster, they returned to save a few belongings. Then bulldozers destroyed what was left.

Hurricane Katrina was the most costly **natural disaster** in the history of the United States. It destroyed about $100 billion worth of homes, businesses, and other property.

Helping to Rebuild

After losing everything in Hurricane Katrina, Alice decided to leave the Mississippi coast. However, many **survivors** wanted to rebuild their homes and their lives.

Former U.S. presidents George H. W. Bush (right) and Bill Clinton (left) raised more than $130 million to help schools, hospitals, and communities recover.

Americans donated more than $1 billion to help the survivors of Hurricane Katrina.

People from across the country gave time and money to help the survivors. For example, Liz McCartney, who lived in Washington State, came to Louisiana after the storm to help with the rebuilding. When she saw the horrible conditions of most homes, she started a group called the St. Bernard Project. Through it, she began organizing **volunteers** and raising money to rebuild the damaged homes. By 2009, Liz and about 17,000 volunteers had helped rebuild 250 houses.

One of those homes belonged to Rudy Aguilar. "Little by little, one house at a time, we'll be back," Rudy said. "I know it."

It takes the St. Bernard Project about 12 weeks and about $15,000 to rebuild each house.

This home is being rebuilt by:

ST BERNARD
P R O J E C T

in participation with United Way

www.stbernardproject.org

A Long, Hard Struggle

A year after Hurricane Katrina struck in 2005, many neighborhoods were still struggling to get back on their feet. A third of all the schools, libraries, and hospitals in New Orleans were closed. So were more than half of the city's restaurants. Poor areas like the Lower Ninth Ward had a particularly tough time recovering.

A year after the hurricane, much of the Lower Ninth Ward was still in ruins.

Hurricane Katrina caused so much damage that scientists retired its name. In the future, no other storms will be called Katrina.

However, there were some good signs. The U.S. government gave more than $7.5 billion to help 120,000 Louisiana families rebuild their houses. Also, on September 25, 2006, the New Orleans Saints football team played its first home game since Hurricane Katrina. The Superdome had a new roof, and it was once again a working stadium.

It took more than two years after Katrina for some New Orleans streetcars to start running again.

The U.S. government provided trailers to people who had lost their homes but wanted to stay in New Orleans.

New Challenges and Old Memories

Cities like New Orleans that lie on a coast will always face hurricanes. So the people who live in them need to plan for future storms. For example, New Orleans and other nearby cities have made plans to improve ways to alert people about possible hurricanes as well as ways to evacuate people by bus before storms strike.

Scientists are also working to protect and restore **wetlands**, which naturally absorb water. Healthy wetlands can soak up much of the storm surge and may help reduce the kind of flooding that destroyed the Lower Ninth Ward.

More than 2,000 square miles (5,180 sq km) of Louisiana's wetlands have disappeared in the last 70 years. These wetlands could have helped protect New Orleans from flooding during Hurricane Katrina.

Crews work on a newly built levee in the Lower Ninth Ward.

These changes will help make people safer in the future. Still, nothing can erase Katrina survivors' terrible experiences and painful memories. "I think of the babies. I think of the elderly," said Brian Williams. "I can't get their faces out of my mind."

A flooded street in New Orleans a few days after Hurricane Katrina hit

Less than a month after Hurricane Katrina, the Gulf Coast faced another tremendous storm. On September 24, 2005, Hurricane Rita struck Texas and Louisiana, after striking the Florida Keys a few days before. Seven people died, and about $10 billion of property was destroyed.

Famous Hurricanes

The United States has a long history of dangerous hurricanes. Here are a few that have resulted in destruction and death.

Galveston, Texas, 1900

- On September 8, 1900, a Category 4 hurricane hit Galveston, Texas. More than 8,000 people were killed by the huge storm surge brought ashore by the hurricane. At the time, it was the deadliest natural disaster the United States ever faced.

Florida, 1992

- On August 24, 1992, Hurricane Andrew slammed into Florida. More than one million people had to evacuate to escape the Category 5 storm's winds and storm surge. Winds of up to 165 miles per hour (266 kph) caused more damage than any other hurricane until Katrina.

Mississippi, Louisiana, and Virginia, 1969

- On August 17, 1969, Hurricane Camille struck Mississippi, Louisiana, and Virginia. Its almost 200-mile-per-hour (322-kph) winds made Camille a strong Category 5 hurricane. The storm and the flooding it caused killed about 250 people.

Damage from Hurricane Andrew

Hurricane Safety

Here are some hurricane safety tips from the Federal Emergency Management Agency:

- ✔ A hurricane watch means that a hurricane is possible in a certain area within 36 hours. During a hurricane watch, listen to the radio or watch television for weather updates. Stay in touch with neighbors about evacuation orders. Make sure there is gas in the car and be ready to leave.
- ✔ A hurricane warning means that a hurricane is expected within 24 hours. During a hurricane warning, be ready to evacuate. If you are advised to evacuate, do so.
- ✔ Always keep a disaster supply kit ready. The kit should include water, food, a flashlight, blankets, and first-aid supplies.
- ✔ Storm shutters are the best protection for windows. If there are no storm shutters, then an adult should board up the outside windows with pieces of wood before the storm. That way, the glass will not break and hurt people.
- ✔ Bring in outside furniture before the storm. An adult should also remove roof antennas and shut off the water, electricity, and gas to prevent leaks and fires.
- ✔ If evacuation is not necessary, then stay indoors during the hurricane. Outside, it's easy to be hit by flying objects. A pause in the wind could be the eye of the storm. Do not go out until the storm has completely passed over your area.
- ✔ If evacuation is necessary, do not go back home until local officials say it is safe to return.

Glossary

atmosphere (AT-muhss-fihr) the mixture of gases that surrounds Earth

breached (BREECHT) broken through

category (KAT-uh-*gor*-ee) a group or division used to classify things

diameter (dye-AM-uh-tur) the distance across a circle in a straight line

evacuated (i-VAK-yoo-*ate*-id) left a dangerous area

eye (EYE) the calm center of a hurricane or tropical storm

eyewall (EYE-wawl) the area just outside the eye of the storm, where thunder and winds are strongest

forecasters (FOR-kast-urz) people who predict what the weather will be in the future

Gulf Coast (GULF KOHST) the area made up of the coasts of Texas, Louisiana, Mississippi, Alabama, and Florida—the states that border the Gulf of Mexico

hurricane (HUR-uh-kane) a circular storm that forms over the ocean with heavy rains and winds of at least 74 miles per hour (119 kph)

inland (IN-luhnd) on land, away from the water

landfall (LAND-fawl) the arrival of a hurricane at dry land from the ocean

levees (LEV-eez) banks made of earth, concrete, or other material, built next to a body of water to prevent flooding

moisture (MOIS-chur) small particles of water

natural disaster (NACH-ur-uhl duh-ZASS-tur) an event caused by weather or nature that results in great damage or loss

storm surge (STORM SURJ) a rise in the level of the ocean caused by a hurricane or tropical storm

surface (SUR-fiss) the top layer

survivors (sur-VYE-vurz) people who live through a disaster or horrible event

tropical storm (TROP-uh-kuhl STORM) a circular storm that forms over the ocean, with heavy rains and winds of between 39 and 73 miles per hour (63 and 117 kph)

victims (VIK-tuhmz) people who are hurt or killed by something or someone

volunteers (vol-uhn-TIHRZ) people who work without pay

water vapor (WAW-tur VAY-pur) water in the form of a gas

wetlands (WET-landz) marshes or other places where the soil is very damp

Bibliography

Brinkley, Douglas. *The Great Deluge: Hurricane Katrina, New Orleans, and the Mississippi Coast.* New York: William Morrow (2006).

Federal Emergency Management Agency. "Hurricanes." www.fema.gov/kids/hurr.htm

Handwerk, Brian. "New Orleans Levees Not Built for Worst Case Events." *National Geographic News* (September 2, 2005). news.nationalgeographic.com/news/2005/09/0902_050902_ katrina_levees.html

Horne, Jed. *Breach of Faith: Hurricane Katrina and the Near Death of a Great American City.* New York: Random House (2006).

Williams, Brian. *In His Own Words: Brian Williams on Hurricane Katrina* (transcript; October 27, 2005). www.msnbc.msn.com/ id/14518359/ns/nightly_news_with_brian_williams-after_katrina

Read More

Langley, Andrew. *Hurricanes, Tsunamis, and Other Natural Disasters.* Boston: Kingfisher (2006).

Latham, Donna. *Hurricane!: The 1900 Galveston Night of Terror.* New York: Bearport (2006).

Torres, John Albert. *Hurricane Katrina and the Devastation of New Orleans, 2005.* Hockessin, DE: Mitchell Lane (2006).

Learn More Online

To learn more about hurricanes, visit
www.bearportpublishing.com/DisasterSurvivors

Index

About the Author

Miriam Aronin is a writer and editor. She also enjoys knitting, dancing, and avoiding natural disasters.